Everyday Prayers for Teens

# EVERYDAY
# PRAYERS
## for
# Teens

Barry L. Culbertson

## DIMENSIONS
### FOR LIVING

NASHVILLE

# EVERYDAY PRAYERS FOR TEENS

*Copyright © 1994 by Dimensions for Living*

96 97 98 99 00 01 02 03—10 9 8 7

This book is printed on acid-free recycled paper.

ISBN 0-687-31694-4

Scripture quotations noted RSV are from the Revised Standard Version of the Bible, copyright 1946, 1952, 1971 by the Division of Christian Education of the National Council of the Churches of Christ in the USA, and are used by permission. Other quotations are the author's paraphrase.

MANUFACTURED IN THE UNITED STATES OF AMERICA

# Contents

# For Using My Time Wisely

Good morning, God. Here I am sitting on the edge of my bed just barely awake. I've got a big test today, and I was up late last night cramming for it. Guess I should have hit the books earlier. This is getting to be a bad habit. I do want to do well in school . . . most of the time. But this last-minute stuff is not working. Help me get my use of time under your guidance. You are a God who cares about the details. And go with me today when I put pencil to paper. I need to think clearly. Guess getting to bed earlier might help! Right, God? Thanks for listening. Amen.

# Words Can Hurt

Oh, God, I've done it again. Gone and made Mom mad at me. She says she's not mad, but she's not talking to me very much. I said something I should have left unsaid. Forgive me. Help her to forgive me. Better still give me the courage to apologize. I find that hard to do. Help me to remember that words can hurt the ones you love and leave a big emotional mess to clean up. God, you are the one who can give me the better words for someone I really love and really didn't want to hurt. Help. Amen.

# For a Perfect Day

God, as I lie here in my bed I praise you for this great day. Food, friends, and fun as the commercial puts it. I had a great day. When good things happen I understand you are underneath or within or behind everything that is good. Thanks! I really enjoy being alive on days like this. It's like a gift that just IS! I realize they can't all be as perfect as this one, so I'll try my best not to take them for granted when they come along. In spite of the bad days (and some are awful! Remember?) I still praise you for the good. Thanks for making good times possible. Praise you and thanks again! Amen!

# For My Body

Dear God, just a quick prayer to tell you how amazed I am. I was watching these college guys play basketball on TV, and I am truly amazed at how great our bodies are. I'm amazed at seeing all the energy and power and speed that we are capable of! What an amazing creation you have put together. Did you have sports in mind when you made us? Maybe not so much sports as just the joy of play. And it's great to have a body (not just a spirit) to enjoy using power and energy and speed. Oh yeah . . . help me take care of this body. Remind me to use it . . . correctly. Amen.

# A Prayer for Driving

God, you saw that. I was making 70 in a 55 mph zone. Gosh how dumb. Forgive me. I can't believe I did that! I know better. What is it about my driving?! I know the rules and the laws. But here I go breaking them. There is so much freedom in being in a car away from home and out here on my own. Why should I want to take such a chance, a risk of blowing this freedom, this independence, this . . . chance to be responsible even when no one is looking over my shoulder? Why abuse this privilege, this freedom? Well, I'm praying to you to help me get my head on straight about this car business. I do want to drive and do want to be responsible. Help me . . . to think! Amen!

# For a Difficult Friend

God, I'm praying about _____. I'm sure you've noticed that she is the most irritating person I've been around lately. I thought she might be a good friend at the first of the school year, but that was a mistake. She will not leave me alone. She's like my shadow and I can't get a word in edgewise when we're with the rest of the gang. I am really getting a bad attitude about her and I need your help. I know I can't ask you to remove her from my life, but that's about the way I feel. Honest! So . . . thanks for listening. This seems so trivial when the world is so messed up, but this has gotten to be a real sore spot in my life. Help me to find the right words and the right attitude about her. Help me do the right thing. The bottom line is, do I have to stay friends with her. Amen.

# A Prayer List

God, here's my list. Each one on the list is very important to me today. I believe you will understand what I mean when I just say the word. OK? I'm praying for:

the neighbor whose wife died
the hungry everywhere
the problem at school
Uncle Bill
my grades
Friday night
the words I said to Jill
that test next week
the money I need

That's about it. Thanks for listening. Do what you can through my prayers. Help me keep my eyes open to the help you give. Thanks. Amen and Amen.

# A Prayer for Snow

God, just a prayer for the snow. Beautiful! Nice work! And a day off from classes! Nice combination! Protect those who have to drive in all this. May they also see how beautiful it is even as they have to come and go in it. Thanks for the fun I intend to have real soon! God bless everyone in the snow! Amen!

# In a World of Hunger

God of every nation and all people, I am saddened by the reports of so many hungry people throughout the world. Yet, I have so much to eat and so many places in which to eat! When I get hungry I know I will find food, but what of those I do not know or will never meet? Remind me of these, your people also, and how I might help by supporting hunger offerings at church, at school, and in the community. "Give us this day, our daily bread. . . ." It has been given and I must find a way to share the bounty of the earth and the labor of our hands. Amen.

# For the Weekend

God of all time and space, here it is Friday and the expression I hear all around me is T.G.I.F. The weekend will be full of activities that you might or might not approve of. I have many choices to make. I ask for your guidance that I might have fun and yet be responsible, not hurting myself or others. Help me to at least include in this "weekend" some "sabbath time." Let me not forget to rejoice and give thanks for rest and leisure, fun, and worship, wherever I am and whatever I do. Amen.

# After "Breaking Up"

O God, I can hardly believe this has happened! We are no longer going together after all this time. This hurts and I feel very strange. I have mixed feelings like "I'm sad and glad," not knowing when I'll feel sad and surprised when I feel glad! Friends have been a help, but they can't possibly feel the emptiness that I am beginning to live with throughout the day. Yet, each day gives me hope that this is not the worst that can happen. I don't believe there could be a "worst" as I believe that you will "not forsake me nor leave me" even when all else around me is falling apart. Help me to give thanks for that which was good about our relationship and I pray that we can someday call each other "friend" once again. With your help, Amen.

# Hurt Feelings

Understanding God, I have been hurt by someone who should have known better. I thought that we were close enough not to hurt each other's feelings. Words do hurt. I feel betrayed and left out. I think about how much pain and rejection Jesus must have felt when his own disciples abandoned him even denying knowing him three times. May I have the faith that Jesus goes with me when others have left me. Amen.

# I Have a Brother

God of every family, I thank you for the wonderful brother who amuses me, cares for me, and drives me crazy sometimes! He makes me laugh at the most unexpected moments, usually when I need a lift. And he treats me as though I count, as though I am capable of great things. Others may call me names, but he calls me "brother." I pray that this day would be wonderful for him as he touches so many lives with his bright spirit and gentleness. I hope there will be more like him in this world. He's your kind of Christian! Amen.

# I Have a Sister

God of every family, I thank you for the delightful sister who makes me laugh, holds me when I cry, and walks with me whether in sunshine or in gloom. She is a beautiful person who radiates love to all those around her. What a gift to our family! What a gift to the world! Bless her throughout this day as she touches so many lives in her daily tasks. Her kindness is surely "the music of life." I hope there will be more like her in your world. She's your kind of Christian! Amen.

# The Lord Is My Friend

The Lord is my friend.
I really do have everything I need.
God gives me plenty of breaks as I get tired
    sometimes.
God sees to it that I can handle the hassles.
The Lord pumps me up when I'm down.
This friend helps me do the right thing.

Even though I see that death does happen
    (and will come to me as well someday),
I'm not really afraid of what comes after;
    God is good.
God is for real here and now, for me here
    and now.
This strong friend has ways to come
    through for me!

I will do well even if people put me down;
God will always give me a safe place to
    come home to.

(The word is that I will eat well and feel
very fine!).

Yes, God is a true and forgiving friend who
plans on being with me forever. Amen.

# For My Teachers

O wise God, hear my prayer for my teachers. I love them today; I couldn't stand them yesterday! I do believe they know what to teach, but their ways are not my ways! Yet, I see them stand before us day in and day out. Some work with us after school in sports, in clubs, in band, even helping late with homework! Lord, hear my prayer for my teachers. Give them more patience, make me more attentive. Help me see past the homework on to what I would like to become because of doing the homework! Lord, hear my prayer for my teachers. Help me see them as, well . . . human like me! Amen.

# For a Bus Trip

O God of the open road, where buses full of students head out on field trips, for football fields, for gyms across the county, go with us. Remind us of the great joy of friendships both new and old; of discoveries of other towns and schools; of museums and auditoriums. Let these be part of our education alongside reading assignments and tests. Thank you for our busdriver and our escort, our teachers and our coaches, our teams and our opponents. Amen.

# For a Coach

God of strength and gentleness, let me offer this prayer for my coach. You know how hard he tries for all of us and what it does to him when we don't try. May I do my very best, enjoy the game, and not worry about winning or losing. And above all may my coach see you in me even if I never say a word about my faith. Amen.

# For Our Youth Meeting

O God, for our youth meeting tonight I pray we will celebrate our coming together as friends for one another and friends for Jesus. This I ask, in his name. Amen.

# Hanging Out

God of every time of day, it's late, after school, and I am hanging out, celebrating just doing nothing. Yes, Lord, we are going to talk, chatter, banter, and be ourselves. I hope. No telling what will be said or who will say it. I try to give you my thoughts, words, and behavior. Have patience with me while I hang out. It's my way, our way, of relaxing. Help me to "watch my step and keep my cool." Amen.

# When Friends Are Not Friendly

O God, words do hurt. _____ criticized me in front of everyone. I can't believe it. What do you do with anger and hurt Lord? I didn't want revenge, I just wish it had never been said! If this is part of growing up and learning to get along, I'm not sure I can handle it. What should I do? Is it just wait and see, or do I ask for an apology? I mean, this person was supposed to my friend! Now I think that I was friends with a jerk. Help me to not see a jerk, but someone who acted unkind and may not do it again, ever. Am I talking about forgiveness? Please let me know. Amen.

# Glad

O God! Refresh me like a cool shower.
Gladden my heart with the joy of a bright
and sunny day. Send the old worries away,
far away, far away; and make glad this
youthful heart! Amen!

# Distant from God

To God through Jesus (who walked with us). How I want to know you, but seeing and hearing you are difficult. You seem so distant, so much like a distant star. I want to believe, but believing is asking a lot from me right now. Yet, I am praying . . . and waiting for your Word Jesus to come and help make a new season of faith come forth. You can do it . . . I believe. In Jesus' name, I pray. Amen.

# I Did Not Go to Church Today

I did not go to church today, O God. The bed was so comfortable and yesterday was so full that to sleep some more seemed to be right. Was I wrong? A day of rest is what I really needed, and I praise you for giving us that Sabbath rest. I slept in while others worshiped, though, and all I can say is . . . next time. Until then let me worship you wherever I am. Praise God! Praise God!

# To Tell Others

I hear, O God, that
You need us to tell others!
You need us to talk about our faith!
You need us to show your love, to make
    Jesus known in us!

I pray I will be part of those who will be
    not only hearers of your Word,
But doers of the Word as well. As Isaiah
    instructed us:
"My witnesses are you says the Lord God
My servant whom I have chosen
To the end that you may take thought
And believe in me (Isaiah 43:10).

# The Church, the Body of Christ

Maker of Heaven and Earth, hear my prayer for the church:

I pray for the church here in this place, and in Russia, India, Canada, Israel, Japan, Australia, Korea, Italy, Zaire, Pakistan, Cuba, Brazil, Burma, Poland, New Zealand, Egypt, China, Iraq, Nepal, Nigeria, Germany, Iceland, Peru, Vietnam, Greece, Libya, Finland, Spain, Colombia, England, Ceylon, Ethiopia, Jamaica, and all the wonderful rest of your world. Christ is with us, around us, in us, and . . . for us! Amen.

# This Rock in My Hand

O God, who created and is creating,
I hold this rock in my hand
And I believe.
Where did it come from? Where will it go?
Small rock, large stone, mountain and val-
    ley.
You made them all and I give you thanks.
I offer this prayer in gratitude for the world
    richly
Gifted with wonders to hold.
O Mighty Rock. Amen, Amen.

# At the Center

O God,
Forgive me
For keeping you just on the outside
Just within sight.
Forgive me for treating you as only a
    Rescuer.
I pray that I would let you in closer
To the center,
To the center of my life. Amen.

# Keeping Score

God of the hurt, God of the overcomers,
I have been hurt again by someone I care
   about.
I want to keep a record of wrongs done to
   me.
I want to keep score.
Remind me that life is not game a of win-
   ners and losers, nor of you-hit-me,
I'll-hit-you. I confess I feel that way, and I
   ask your forgiveness.
Help me always to see the "big picture"
   when people are hard to get along with.
In the name of the One who understands.
   Amen.

# For Grandparents

Thank you God, for my grandparents. They may have some "age" on them, but they are still great to have around! I hope they can be here for years to come. There are not that many people who really love me like they do . . . unconditionally! Amen.

# Telephone

Thanks be to you, O God, the one who speaks and listens. Thanks be to you who gives us speech and hearing. If only I would use both to build up others and not tear down. You know I spend a lot of time on the phone with friends. I hear more gossip than good news. But, sometimes I am able to be helpful, because some friend can reach me *only* by phone! "Let the words of my mouth and the meditation of my heart, be acceptable in thy sight, O LORD, my rock and my redeemer" (Psalm 19:14 RSV).

# Camping Out

O Creator God, the one who made and is making, bless us in this camp, in these magnificent woods, near such green, open fields. These are places to bless and in which to be blessed. May we use and not abuse, may we preserve and not destroy because we have been here.

O Maker of Heaven and Earth, how wonderful are your works; for blue skies, for oceans without oil spills; for fewer endangered species and greater wetlands, for nature wild, yet in your hands, this we pray. Amen.

# Sunrise and Sunset

For what I see, red and yellow, and pink and blue, and orange and purple, O Lord, I give thanks and say "Good work, God." Your name be blessed forever. Amen.

# God Is

God is! What a statement! Let this be my prayer: GOD IS. May I meditate upon GOD IS and let such wonder fill me; let such a thought amaze me, and give me peace. Amen.

# The TV Remote

O God beyond our technology,
yet, the one who makes all things possible,
As I "range" from channel to channel help
    guide my decisions
In what to watch. May I enjoy the gifts of
    creativity and imagination,
Action and adventure, suspense and
    humor. But, let me be careful in that
which would encourage me to despair or
    make acceptable that which degrades
And dehumanizes. May TV entertain but
    not bring me to accept values that
Make us less than you intend. Amen.

# Peer Pressure

O God of a world full of beer, cigarettes, drugs, teen sex, fast cars, and fast-lane living, you are the One who points us to health and abundant living. I pray that I will use and not abuse my life. I pray that I can listen as much to you as to TV commercials and peer pressure. And I pray for my friends (especially some of them) . . . who may not listen as well as they should. Amen.

# Prejudice

O God, remind me: "Red and yellow, black and white, they are precious in his sight . . ." whenever I am tempted to prejudice. I hope I will never be too old to sing this song. "Jesus loves the little children of the world." Amen.

# Money

O God, help me to keep my needs simple so that when I pray for money it will be for others who really need it! And when I do have money make me wise in the "ways of the world" giving more and spending less. "With God all things are possible!" (Matthew 19:26 RSV). Amen.

# Music and Tears

O God of many melodies and rhythms, I heard a song today that made me cry. Before the day was over I was giving thanks for the joy of music. May this happen more often. Amen.

# The Dog, the Cat, and More

O Creator of creatures "great and small," hear my prayer of thanks for the "fur" at my feet! They give such joy when they run, frolic, purr, bark, lick, chase, dig, sleep, and sleep some more. Companions on an earthly journey giving happiness to the other creatures you made but a "little lower than the angels." Could it be that heaven is theirs also? I would hope so "that my joy would be made complete." Thanks be to God. Amen.

# Tonight Is Date Night

Lord of all my life, here I go on a date, tonight, this night. Nervous, but looking forward to fun, to getting to know someone new (sorta). Words come to my mind. You know what I mean. When I think of intimacy, let me not forget respect; when I think of romance, remind me of a place for genuine love. As we drive, if we dance, when we talk (and when we don't), be there for us, quietly, silently, be there. Amen.

# Buying a Gift

O Giver of all good gifts, I'm going shopping today. I want to buy the best (not the most expensive) gift for this person I name before you: _____. I want to find a gift that somehow shows us how much I feel toward this person. I want to make the purchase personal, I want to find something . . . from the heart. Give me patience as I search and wisdom as I decide. And remind me; not the amount of money, nor the name of the store, nor the brand count for anything, if I do not purchase to give joy to the other and to reflect our relationship. Now . . . let's go shop! Amen.

# God, I Told a Joke Today

God, I told a joke today. It got a lot of laughs. I impressed my friends. But, I put somebody down in the joke. Where do we draw the line on humor? I need to think this one through. I need to know the difference between laughing at someone and laughing with someone. People can be funny at times can't they? Can we laugh without hurting someone? Help me in my humor, O you who must know what it is to laugh! Amen.

# Just Praise

On the mountain,
in the valley,
by the sea, on the shore;
on the dance floor,
in the back yard,
near the football field,
on the court;
in the church,
in the classroom,
on the job,
and while asleep;
watching TV,
"kicking back,"
holding hands,
and slapping backs;
in quiet
and with stereo booming,
in sickness,
and in health,
whether sad or glad,
your name be praised! Amen!

# No Answer . . . Today?

I prayed today and no answer came.
I wonder.

I wait. I believe. I trust.

God, "I believe; help Thou my unbelief!"
  (Mark 9:24b)

# Bad Moods

O God, keep me from a bad mood, moodiness, and that all-bad attitude.

Lord, I can be irritable, grouchy, grumpy, whiny, and negative.

This is not the abundant life you promised (John 10:10).

I make no excuses for the way my life has gone lately, but I do seek the changes faith can make in me as I step toward the future you hold.

O God, forgive me of my bad attitude and help me shape up, grow up, and go on. I can do better . . . with your help. Glory be to God. Amen!

# I Struck Out

O God of great energy and great re-
creation, hear my sadness please. Today I
struck out with a runner on third. We
went on to lose the game and no one felt
worse than I did. I struck out with the
tying run at third. O Lord, what a low day!

I pray instead of cursing as I know you care
    about my feelings and what I do with
    them. Win or lose you are with me.

Lord, I struck out! Hear my prayer.

I'll play again and I'll strike out again; but
    Lord . . . I do hope there is no one on
    third! Amen.

# It's Monday

O God, it's Monday again. First, let me share with you the bad news: I'm still sleepy from staying up late, I don't have all my work done, and it looks like I will not get it finished. My body aches also. Now the good news: I rejoice for this is the day the Lord has made and I am alive. I can start over once more and do good work before the week is over. I can "call upon the name of the Lord and be helped." I can look forward and not backward. I can "seek first the Kingdom of God" and other important things will follow along as needed. "I can do all things through Christ who strengthens me." O God, I believe the good news outweighs the bad news! Thanks be to God. Amen.

# A New Thing

God, Creator who is still creating, help me be more aware of the new things you are doing in my life and throughout the world. I am so used to thinking of you and "church," that I overlook your presence all around me. The "church" is more than Sunday mornings in a beautiful building. You are everywhere and at all times. How could I miss you?! And when I *do* miss you (as I will) forgive me, guide me, and "pull me along" if you have to. Through Jesus Christ, who is doing a new thing in my life, Amen.

# Daily Bread

O Great Provider,
if I understand what "give us this day
our daily bread" means then surely I need
not worry about "what I will eat or what I
will wear" each day. God, help me from
getting caught up in the *fashions and fast
food* of my age. Thank you for the basics
and remind me that many in the world still
go without their daily bread. Help me *want*
to make a difference for the better . . .
while I can. Amen.

# My Car

O God, my car needs repairs and I don't have the money right now. I really like my car as I think of the freedom and power and independence it has given me. It will be several days before it is fixed. I pray that I will be patient and think about other ways that I can receive and learn about real freedom (in Christ) and real power (through the Holy Spirit) and the fact that independence is not as important as being part of a loving, caring family of God. O God, I really *like* my car; may I really *love* you and those around me. (Thank you God that prayers can start with *anything* and include most *everything!*) Praise be to the Father, and to the Son, and to the Holy Spirit. Amen.

# House Duties

O God, lover of families,
O God, the one who blesses homes,
Go with me through these daily tasks:
the dirty clothes,
the dirty dishes,
the trash,
the cat litter,
the pets and their food,
the beds unmade,
the bathrooms,
the clothes on the floor and shoes under
    the couch,
the carpets and the rugs,
the bills,
the dust on the shelves,
the uncut yard,
the unswept walkway,
and the one or two chores I forgot!
O God, lover of families,
O God, the one who blesses homes,
Go with me . . . Amen.

# The Lord's Supper

O God,
Before I receive the bread and the cup,
Help me remember (always this if nothing
    else)
I'm eating and drinking with Jesus
Eating and drinking with Jesus
With Jesus
Jesus.
In the name of the Father, and the Son,
    and the Holy Spirit. Amen.

# When I Go to Sleep

"Now I lay me down to sleep,
I pray the Lords my soul to keep."
Thanks be to God that I can still say this
　　and believe it,
And believe your swirling planets and
　　galaxies will still be there when I wake;
And your distant stars will stay and
　　brighten our way;
And the "earth is the Lord's and the full-
　　ness therein;"
And the animal and plant kingdom will
　　greet me in the day (after rest for all);
And that the song of the birds will be with
　　me as I rise from my bed.
Thanks be to God that I can say this and
　　believe it.
Peace be with me and with the world.
Amen.

# Slow Me Down

God of infinite stillness,
   Slow me down from my day-rush, head-
strong, olympic life. Show me the value of
a pace closer to the rhythm of your Word.
Remind me that Jesus went to quiet places,
prayed, and came again to his friends so
that he could really be with and for his
friends. Slow me down that I might listen
. . . to my heart, to my life, to the Source
of all life. God of infinite stillness, slow me
down. Amen.

# If I Fail

If I fail, O Divine Friend, will you be
there? When I fail, Guiding Holy Light,
will you understand my weakness and sin?
I have failed, Forgiving One, many times
and yet you never leave me. You believe in
me. You encourage me. I can try again.
Thanks be to God. Amen.

# Ready to Drive

O God who travels with us, hear my prayer of preparation: seatbelt buckled, ignition, hands-on-the-wheel, defensive driving state-of-mind, speed limits in mind, thoughts of responsibility for others. Hear my prayer, O God of the miles ahead. Amen.

# Visiting Another Church

God of all peoples, this is different in sight and sound; people standing here when we would have been sitting; songs that I have never heard. But, Lord, help me to listen, help me to see, help me to find your Good News with these your people too. It's for everybody . . . right?! Amen.

# A Prayer Before Praying

O God of great silence who speaks a Word, I will be silent now (for as long as it takes) before I begin my prayers of praise or confession or thanks or requests. Praying needs some peace and quiet don't you think? Amen.

# Teach Us to Pray

My caring Parent who is heavenly (but not
 far away),
Absolutely great is your name.
Bring us the best life together with you,
And what you would have us do, let us get
 on with it in this world!
May no one go hungry (including me):
 food for the body and food for our
 spirits.
Forgive all of us for the hurts we cause
 others (and you). Help us forgive others
 who have hurt us as well. May we be
 spared the temptation to do wrong,
 and, in spite of the worst that can
 happen, get through this life knowing
 you will be there for us, with us, and in
 us. When all is said and done, it is your
 world, you have the loving power, and
 you *are* forever! Amen!

# For a Great Day

O Lord, what a great, magnificent, wonderful day! I'm alive and thankful! What more can I say? I can't because I just *feel* it! Thanks again! Amen.

# If Only

If only today God,
No guns would blaze,
No hearts would ache,
No tears would fall,
No graves would be dug.
If only today God,
Wounds would heal,
The deaf would hear,
The blind would see,
The weak would run.
If only today God,
I could help these come true,
Then heaven God, then heaven.
Amen.

# Jump Start Me, Lord

Jump start me, Lord, as my spiritual battery
   is real low.
Send in your servant mechanics; surprise
   me with the price:

*Special Today and Tomorrow and Forever—*
   *Free! Courtesy of All Night, All Day,*
   *Always Wrecker Service.*

Jump start me, Lord, as my spiritual battery
   is real low. Amen.

# Cookies and Milk

Thanks for the memories, God, of cookies and milk, brought by loving hands with a warm smile. I remember. It was not that long ago. Cookies and milk set before me as I watched my favorite TV show. The room was bright with caring . . . and cookies and milk. Thanks. (Later, can I take this memory with me to heaven? There ought to be a lot of good memories there!) Amen.

# Doubt

Thank you, Lord, for doubt. It must be a backroad to faith for I have driving on it for sometime now. But, I just came through the intersection called "community of faith" and I started to recognize my way once more. Thanks be to God. Amen.

# Rock Music

O God of music and imagination, this is the music of my generation and it is full of energy. I pray that I will be wise in knowing what to take with me and what to leave behind when I listen to guitar and amp, bass and drums, organ and saxophone. If there is a message in the rhythm and beat, may it affirm life, give me joy and make me think (after I stop dancing!). Amen.

# For Understanding Scripture

God, I just finished reading some difficult passages of scripture. I don't believe I understood anything. I picked up my Bible and turned to the book of Romans. I was lost after a few chapters. Funny I should use the word "lost." I've heard that before in sermons and with some of the TV preachers. But, couldn't you and the writers of the Bible have been a little clearer in what you wanted us to know? I mean I can follow passages like the 23rd Psalm and John 3:16, but other places (like Romans) I just can't get the point. I think I better keep it simple so I don't get frustrated or lose interest. But, I'll keep trying. I think I understand about "seeking, and knocking, and asking." And I'll try to pay more attention at church. Be patient with me. Thanks. And Amen.

# I Start Work Today

O God, whose work is through the Living Word, bless me as I begin a new job today: It could be brooms, mops, shovels, tools of a trade; it might be trucks, carts, boxes, bags, or computers, typewriters, paper and pens. O God, whose work is through the Body of Christ, bless me this day, as I know for sure there will be people in need, people to serve. Amen.

# Flowers

O artist God of all creation, I thank you for the delicate colors and patterns which brighten my dinner table, our dinner table. They remind me of your infinite creativity and playfulness with nature. I pray that our human lives will reflect that creativity, that brightness, that life you so freely give to all. Remind me to share this sample of beauty . . . perhaps on the table of my neighbor, my friends, the lonely and the hurt. You give beauty to all . . . to be shared. Amen.

# Silent Prayer in a Restaurant

O God,
for family, friends, and food;
thanks be to thee for all three. Amen.

# In Between

Lord,
I'm in between a lot of things. I'm feeling
   like I'm crossing a bridge but I'm not sure
   where I've been and where I'm going. I
   feel older, but still young; wiser, but not
   wise. I'm in between. Almost like being
   squeezed through a narrow gate.
Lord,
I'm in between.
Find me a full-color map, a frontier guide,
   a trail bike for the spirit.
Lord,
I'm in between. Leaving home, but want-
   ing a place to call home; wanting to be
   on my own, but with others I can trust
   and love.
Lord,
I'm in between. Help me find the Way,
   O "pioneer and perfecter of our faith."
   Amen.

# Love Never Lets Go

Thank you God, for not letting go. The scripture says you have a tight grip on my life, now and forever (Romans 8:38, 39). How could I not be happy and secure even on bad days? Your love accepts me as I am right here and right now, no strings attached. I pray, O perfect Friend, that my response to this Good News would be faith and a real freedom to love others as you have loved me. And I pray for your forgiveness and continued acceptance when I do fail to love as I should. Thank you God for the example and presence of Jesus who loved and is loving, who was so human and so divine, who will never let us go. Love to Jesus. Amen.

# A Part of the Whole

O God of Abraham, God of Isaac, God
of Jacob, one who has no beginning and
no end, one who is from everlasting to
everlasting:
Remind me of the long history of your
people which includes my own history
of parents, and grandparents and back-
wards through many generations, many
witnesses to faith. Thank you, Lord, that
they came to believe, they worshiped,
they read the scriptures, "they cared for
justice, loved mercy, and walked humbly
with you" (Micah 6:8). I am part of this
great "team of faith," this forgiven
people, this part of your whole creation.
Remind me: I'm not the center, but an
eternally important part of the whole.
Amen.

# Holidays

O gift-giving God,
I thank you for Christmas, the coming of
    eternal joy, the gift of the Father-God.
I thank you for Easter, life over death, the
    gift of the risen Christ.
I thank you for Pentecost, new life in the
    Spirit, the gift of the Holy Spirit.
I thank you for all times and seasons, sum-
    mer, fall, winter, spring, the gift of life.
O gift-giving God, I give you thanks.
    Glory to God in the highest. Amen.

# First Prayer in the Morning

God of day, God of night,
God of morning bright,
I'm alive,
I'm awake.
Let's be up and ready to create!
Amen!

# Something More

O One who "makes all things new,"
I'm looking for something more,
Something more than the "high" of spirts,
Something more than the "glamour" of the
   right clothes,
Something more than the "thrill" of the
   fast car,
Something more than the "glow" of my
   favorite TV show,
Something more than the "talk" of the
   day,
Something more than what I can only
   "touch, taste, and smell."
Maybe that something is more like Some-
   one.
Yes, Someone . . . Amen.

# Right Side Up

O God of still waters and stormy seas,
When my boat of life overturns,
Turn me right side up and anchor me in
    your safe harbor,
Until I am ready to sail forth again in the
    adventure of the next blue-sky day.
Amen.

# No Answers,
# Better Questions

O God of joyful Mystery,
I hoped for an answer to my question
    today.
I didn't see, hear, feel one . . . yet.
O God who also speaks to us through
    silence;
Lead me to better questions if no answers
    . . . yet! Amen.

# Prayer of Abraham Ibn Ezra

Wheresoe'er I turn mine eyes
Around on earth or toward the skies,
I see Thee in the starry field,
I see Thee in the harvest's yield,
in every breath, in every sound,
An echo of thy name is found.
The blade of grass, the simple flower,
Bear witness to Thy matchless pow'r.
My every thought, Eternal God of Heaven,
Ascends to Thee, to whom all praise be
   given.

Abraham Ibn Ezra (1090-1164)

# A Prayer for All Times

"The Lord bless you and keep you:
The Lord make his face to shine upon you,
and be gracious to you:
The Lord lift up his countenance upon
    you,
and give you peace."

Numbers 6:24-26 RSV

# Let Us with a Gladsome Mind

Let us, with a gladsome mind,
Praise the Lord, for He is kind;
For His mercies still endure,
Ever faithful, ever sure.

All things living
he doth feed,
His full hand supplies their need:

Let us with a gladsome mind
Praise the Lord, for he is kind.

John Milton

# Table Graces

Let us in peace eat the food that God has
provided for us. Praise be to God for all his
gifts. Amen.

May the abundance of this table never fail
and never be less, thanks to the blessings
    of
God, who has fed us and satisfied our
    needs.
To him be the glory for ever. Amen.

Prayers of the Armenian Apostolic Church.
The first is to be said before meals, and the second
after meals.

# From the New England Primer

Let all of us,
   in full accord,
Give grateful thanks
   unto the Lord—
A very kind
   and gracious Lord,
Who gives us more
   than our reward.

*New England Primer*

# Feed Our Souls

Great God, we praise your gracious care,
You do our daily bread prepare;
O bless the earthly food we take
and feed our souls, for Jesus' sake. Amen.

John Cennick, 1741

# Christ, Be with Me

Christ, be with me, Christ before me,
Christ behind me,
Christ in me, Christ beneath me, Christ
above me,
Christ on my right, Christ on my left.
Christ when I lie, Christ when I sit, Christ
when I arise,
Christ in the heart of every one who
thinks of me,
Christ in the mouth of every one who
speaks of me,
Christ in every eye that sees me.
Christ in every ear that hears me.
Salvation is of the Lord,
Salvation is of the Lord,
Salvation is of the Christ,
May your salvation, O Lord, be ever
with us. Amen.

St. Patrick
*Fifth Century*

# Daily Prayer of Thomas Aquinas

Grant me, I beseech Thee, O merciful God, prudently to study, rightly to understand, and perfectly to fulfill that which is pleasing to Thee, to the praise and glory of Thy name.
Thou, O Christ, art the King of glory;
Thou art the everlasting Son of the Father.
Amen.

Thomas Aquinas
*Thirteenth Century*